How to
Grow Rich by Giving

Why Philanthropy Will Multiply Your Wealth

By

Praveen Kumar & Prashant Kumar

Disclaimer

The advice contained in this material might not be suitable for everyone. The author obtained the information from sources believed to be reliable and from his own personal experience, but he neither implies nor intends any guarantee of accuracy.

The author, publisher and distributors never give legal, accounting, medical or any other type of professional advice. The reader must always seek those services from competent professionals that can review their own particular circumstances.

The author, publisher and distributors particularly disclaim any liability, loss, or risk taken by individuals who directly or indirectly act on the information contained herein. All readers must accept full responsibility for their use of this material.

All pictures used in this book are for illustrative purposes only. The people in the pictures are not connected with the book, author or publisher and no link or endorsement between any of them and the topic or content is implied, nor should any be assumed. The pictures are only licensed

Table of contents

Introduction

"The meaning of life is to find your gift. The purpose of life is to give it away."

Pablo Picasso

Have you ever wondered why Bill Gates has pledged 95% and Warren Buffet 99% of their wealth away to charity?

Have you also wondered why Bill Gates continues to be the richest man in the world after having donated over $38 billion to his foundation? His wealth continues to grow at an ever-increasing pace even as he donates.

Bill Gates and Warren Buffet are not alone; there are other billionaires who have pledged to give a major part of their wealth to charity. These include Microsoft cofounder Paul Allen, Manoj Bhargava the founder and CEO of 5-Hour Energy, Spanx founder Sara Blakely, Patrice Motsepe founder of the mining company African Rainbow Minerals, Virgin Group founder Richard Branson, The chairman of Indian consulting and IT company Wipro Azim Premji, Facebook founder and CEO Mark Zuckerberg. The list of these great individuals is simply too long to include here.

This brings us to the question "Is there a co-relation between giving money to charity and becoming richer?" Have these billionaires found some secret to wealth creation that we don't know. Can we apply the same principles to increase our net worth?

We don't learn this from wealth creators alone. Every religious book that I have read or spiritual leader I have met teach that in act of giving we truly receive. We can be cynical about religion or spiritual practices but we simply cannot deny the teaching or the evidence.

The charitable give out the door and God puts it back through the window.

—Traditional proverb

Every wealth creation book that I have read, seminars I have attended or knowledge gained from mentors emphasize the fact that giving leads to wealth creation. I certainly know this from my experience in life: whenever I gave, I received and whenever I was stingy, some misfortune happened in my financial life.

Let us examine some research findings on this subject.

Research

Logically speaking it does not make any sense as to why giving away your hard-earned money should result in increase of wealth. However, research on co-relation between giving and increase in wealth by Arthur C. Brooks of American social scientist and president of the American Enterprise Institute shows that there is connection between the two.

Arthur analyzed data from SCCBS *(The Social Capital Community Benchmark Survey).* The data included a survey of about 30,000 people of different education background, race, age, religion in over 40 communities in the U.S. They were also from various socio-economic backgrounds. The survey revealed the following:

- The people who gave money to charity made more money than those who did not.

- Giving increased by 7% when wealth increased by 10%. This means as a person got richer he could give more.

- People who volunteered for social causes made more money than those who did not.

- Charitable impulse of volunteering made these individuals donate more money than others.

- Giving is about charitable impulse and not only about money. You can get the same results by donating time, sharing knowledge, giving food or for that matter blood.

In his final Analysis, Arthur found that regardless of income, a family who gave away $100 more than another family, in the same earning bracket, earned on an average $375 more than the other family as a result of generosity. He found that this was also true for the organizations and countries that gave away money to charity. In the past 50 years, the per capita of Americans has risen by 150% with an increase in donation of 190% within the same time frame.

This finding is supported by that of data from **Statistical Abstract of United States.** $100 in giving away resulted in an increase of GDP by more than $1800. America being one of the most charitable nations has benefited by being one of the richest.

Sir John Templeton, investor and one of the greatest pioneer of mutual funds of 20th Century stated **"*I have observed 100,000 families over my years of investment counselling. I always saw greater prosperity and happiness among those families who tithed than among those who didn't.*"**

There seems to be some logic in these findings after all! Statistical evidence bears witness to the fact that giving leads to more wealth. But we still need to explore as to why this happens.

Why Giving Leads to Wealth

There are various reasons as to why giving leads to wealth. Some are intuitive and others supported through research.

Sense of Wealth Increases through Act of Giving

Zoe Chance of Yale University and Michael Norton of Harvard Business School, in their research 'I Give, Therefore I Have,' observed the act of giving increases the giver's 'Sense of Wealth.' The giver psychologically feels wealthier than they actually are through the act of giving. This change in mind-set leads to more wealth. Winston Churchill intuitively supported this theory *"We make a living by what we get, but we make a life by what we give."*

Please check out what some of the donors say in their words:

Ted Turner, the founder of CNN: *"Being generous always made I feel great, and it seemed like every time I gave money away, I somehow made that much more."*

Ackman hedge fund billionaire: *"Over the years, the emotional and psychological returns I have earned from charitable giving have been enormous. The more I do for others, the happier I am. The happiness and optimism I have obtained from helping others are a big part of what keeps me sane."*

Mobile phone entrepreneur John Caudwell: *"Philanthropy gives me far more pleasure and satisfaction than making money. In fact, making money is now largely driven by the knowledge that I will be able to leave even more wealth behind for charitable causes when I go."*

Hedge fund billionaire Tom Stayer: *"Surely the pleasure we derive from... consoling, understanding, loving, giving and pardoning far outweigh any selfish and passive pleasures of owning, having, or possessing."*

Michael Bloomberg, founder of Bloomberg: *"Making a difference in people's lives – and seeing it with your own eyes – is perhaps the most satisfying thing you'll ever do. If you want to fully enjoy life, give."*

Hedge fund billionaire John Arnold: *"There is no more worthwhile work and no greater mission [than philanthropy]."*

Here's a quote from the book "Start Late, Finish Rich" by David Bach:

"Over the years, I've spent a lot of time studying the rich and the superrich. The more I've learned, the more I've become convinced that most people who achieve great wealth have at least one thing in common – giving.

When I first heard the billionaire investor and philanthropist Sir John Templeton make this point, I wondered if it could really be true. Could the secret to being rich really be as simple as "give more and more will come back to you"? Does giving really attract wealth?

Some 10 years later, I can say that I am certain of it. Time and again, I've come across examples of superrich individuals who made a point of donating a portion of their earnings to charity – even before they became rich. Indeed, virtually every self-made billionaire I've ever studied echoes Templeton in declaring that tithing or giving was a principle of their life well before they had any money.

As a result, I've come to believe that giving of your time or money to help others is more that the "golden rule." It is the golden magnet. I have seen this happen in my own life and in the lives of hundreds of people around me. It's a simple, observable fact: Those who give lead more abundant lives.

This sums up my thoughts, beliefs, and experiences as well. In fact, I've commented that in the years that I've given the most, I've seen the largest increases in my net worth. It's not a coincidence in my opinion.

This doesn't mean that we give to get more. Really, our motivation should be to help others and that's why we should give. Then, as we're blessed even more financially, that allows us to give even more – and the cycle goes on and on this way."

Increase in Happiness Index and Productivity

The act of giving to under-privileged leads to inner fulfilment which in turn increases the happiness index of a person. Statistics have shown that a happy person is more productive. When a person is more productive it leads to higher levels of earning and wealth.

Studies show that act of giving lowers stress levels. People with low stress levels are more productive and successful. A relaxed person generally has better health, happiness index is higher and they're more successful. Giving creates strong communities. A charitable person will eventually profit from it even though he did not desire it.

Highest of human motivation, according to Maslow's hierarchy, is self-actualization. This is taught in every business class. Just before Maslow died, he put self-transcendence one step beyond self-actualization. According to him, the greatest fulfilment comes when a person seeks a benefit beyond what is personal. He called it self-transcendence – when one's own needs are put aside for service to others, which provides the ultimate fulfilment and happiness. This level of motivation leads to highest productivity.

When we do any good to others, we do as much, or more, well to ourselves.

—Benjamin Whichcote

The act of giving creates psychological changes within a person. Researchers have found that the act of giving stimulates parts of your brain associated with fulfilment of basic needs and primal instincts. Once the brain feels that our fundamental needs are met, it becomes more productive; our decision-making skills, including financial decisions, improve.

Studies also show that giving stimulates empathy and compassion. You tend to become more confident as a person. These subtle changes in personality traits are observed by people around you. They will perceive you as a kind and gentle human being. They will invariably gravitate towards you. They recognize leadership qualities in services to others. Servant leadership is the new mantra to success whether one plans it that way or not. When people see you giving, it inspires them – they cannot help but help you. You will be viewed as a natural leader amongst people and your voice will be heard. These are simple by-products of act of giving and will indirectly result in making you a happier and successful person.

Giving Starts the Receiving Process

The act of giving starts the receiving process. Have you ever tried to receive money with your fists closed? This is simply not possible. If you are hurt after a broken relationship and shut down your heart for fear of pain then you are not in a position to receive love from even the most beautiful and loving person on the planet. You have to open your heart in spite of fear of pain to receive love again. Similarly, if your mind is closed then you are not in the right frame to receive wonderful thoughts that may transform your life forever. The act of giving not only opens your hands, but also your mind and heart. Once you give, you are in a position to receive great wealth. You have to keep your heart, mind and palm open to receive great gifts of life.

"The more doors you open, the more you will allow the universe the opportunity to bring something to you and in ways you could never have imagined."

Anonymous

This is something I can share from my own experience of life: whenever I was stingy, it invariably led to some financial catastrophe in my life. When I observed this fact repeatedly in my life, I forced myself to give even when I found myself in most difficult financial situations. I never wavered in my support of under-privileged children I was educating or refuse anyone who asked me for help in worst of financial times. Providence would always come to my rescue. This magic has never failed.

There is always an ebb and flow of money in our lives. Give when you have cash in hand. Give even more when you are low in money and see the magic happen. I can't prove it scientifically, but it happens. Just try this simple recipe and it will do wonders to your financial health. In every action we take in our lives there is an element of luck involved. Ask any successful person; once you get into the habit of giving the element of luck for some strange reason will favor you.

Law of Cause and Effect

Whether it is physics that explains the law of cause of cause and effect, or spiritual laws of karma that say *"We reap what we sow,"* no one can escape it. David Cameron Gikandi rightfully says *"Give cheerfully and freely. It is the energy behind giving that matters so do not give grudgingly. The law of cause and effect guarantees that you shall receive plenty for what you give."*

Pitanjali, an ancient Indian philosopher, explained this fact a bit differently. He said that there is no linear motion in this universe—everything moves in a circle: planets rotate around the sun, the moon circles the Earth, the Earth rotates around its axis, water rises from the seas becomes cloud, the rain water forms rivers and flows back into the sea completing the full circle. A tree rises from the earth and when it perishes, it goes back to the earth. Man is formed from five elements of the earth and goes back to those elements after death. Good or bad, deeds come back to us in some form whether we realize or not. Similarly, when you give money away it will always come back to you – this is the universal law of nature that no one can escape. Sometimes in our greed, we fail to see the implications of this law. Most enlightened wealth creators understand this basic fact and act according to this law.

Giving Increases Size of Your Network

Although giving is not done with an aim of any monetary benefit, it generates goodwill in hearts and minds of people. It is like a certificate of good health and many people and businesses will like to partner or associate with you.

Bill Ackman, hedge fund billionaire has stated that *"While my motivations for giving are not driven by a profit motive, I am quite sure that I have earned financial returns from giving money away. Not directly by any means, but as a result of the people I have met, the ideas I have been exposed to, and the experiences I have had as a result of giving money away. A number of my closest friends, partners and advisers I met through charitable giving. Their advice, judgment and partnership have been invaluable in my business and in my life. Life becomes richer, the more one gives away."*

There is also inherent fun and joy in giving that brings people together. Ask this question to donors, activists and volunteers and they will tell you about the sense of happiness and camaraderie that happens when people work together for a nobler cause than personal gain. By giving your time, effort or money you increase your circle of influence. You meet diverse and interesting people. As your network grows, so will your wealth.

How Much Money to Give Your Children?

This question is relevant to wealthy parents. How much money to leave to your children?

Most wealthy parents are concerned about the impact of too much unearned wealth on lives of their children. They want their children to lead significant, meaningful and productive lives. They don't want their wealth to come in the way to hurt them. They want to help their children and provide them with adequate financial security but too much wealth can hurt their productivity – it is a very fine and difficult balance.

Most of the super-rich are leaving only fraction of their money to their children. Warren Buffett when asked this question offered a good rule of thumb: *"enough money so that they would feel they could do anything, but not so much that they could do nothing."*

Other rich parents take a completely different view. "Shark Tank" investor and self-made millionaire Kevin O'Leary's has taken a more severe approach. According to him, *"I'm not planning on giving my kids any of my wealth. They know when their education is over; I'm pushing them out of the nest. You want to prepare your children for launching their own lives. I tell wealthy parents that if they don't kick their kids out of the house and put them under the stresses of the real world, they will fail to launch."*

How much money to leave to the kids is a very philosophical question which each parent has to address individually depending upon their situation? No single rule is applicable. One has to understand the nature and capability of their children. Are they wealth creators? Can they handle money? Will they put money to good use or destroy your hard-earned wealth? Will too much money have a corrupting influence or will they use it wisely to enhance their lives and those around them? Parents have to ask these questions of them before deciding on amount of wealth they leave to their children.

Best Way to Give Wealth Away

The best way to give charity is to not make the receiver feel belittled in any way. A self-respecting person can feel humiliated when receiving handouts. The idea is to help a person overcome their problem so that they do not have to be supported for long.

A plant can never grow in shadow of a big tree. Your help should be to make the receiver stand in the sunlight of success. They should never feel beholden to you for help.

There are eight levels of charity.... The highest is when you strengthen a man's hand until he need no longer be dependent upon others.

—Maimonides

The aim of charity should be to help a person become strong so that they become capable and no longer dependent on others. Help should be given without destroying their self-respect.

Monetary help given without proper advice or support is never long lasting. For example, one of the most popular charities is paying for educational support of under-privileged children in third world countries. This is because education changes lives and is the biggest leverage to success. Educating a girl child is even more effective because it changes not only one person but affects the lives of an entire family. However, giving money for child education support is not effective without involving the parents, community and environment around the child.

Andrew Carnegie, one of the richest men of all time (1835 – 1919), gave away 90% of his fortune – around $350 million – to charities, foundations and universities. He did not recommend wealth to be distributed in small quantities as it resulted in waste. Carnegie suggested supporting larger projects such libraries, schools and foundations which he felt brought greater good to humanity.

Carnegie also strongly recommended the rich to live modestly, provide moderately to dependents and use surplus wealth in ways that bring good to community. He spent the last eighteen years of his live devoted to administering charities.

Whenever you decide to give to charity, you must thoroughly research the project; there are many charitable projects that are total waste of your money. In some cases, the administration costs of a project are so high that very little benefit reaches the beneficiary. The charitable organization becomes an end in itself. There are also fraudsters who are only in it to make gain for them.

The best way to give your money is to become involved in the charity of your choice so that you can make a difference. In case you do not have the time, at least make the effort of analyzing the charity and getting feedback from reliable sources before donating money. Giving money away is not as easy as it looks – it takes knowledge, time and effort.

One way is to be sensitive to people and the environment around us. You will be able to find people who need your help. We can't change the whole world but we can definitely influence a few lives within our sphere of influence.

"Wealth is your servant, and you are a servant to your wealth. Money is little more than a tool that comes with a responsibility to use it wisely."

Charity also means taking responsibility for the wealth we create. It should be created without exploiting people and by giving them a fair wage for their work. It also involves taking care of schooling of children of the staff we employ, providing them with housing and health insurance. Also, in the process of creating wealth, we should not cause damage to the environment, which is the immediate sphere of influence. It is charity if we are sensitive and take care of our sphere of influence.

Transcendental Wealth

Most enlightened wealth creators understand that wealth flows, and nobody can block its flow. We are mere custodians of money for a short span of time. It invariably passes through our hands to those of others. No one has been able to take their wealth with them. We pass it to our loved ones or give it to charity. Some fools try and guard it closely only to leave legacy of legal battles when they die. Wealth continues to flow whether we like it or not.

What we do with the wealth when we are custodians for a limited period of time is what matters. Wealth is a privilege and great responsibility. It takes much lesser effort and knowledge to make money than to spend it wisely. It needs great wisdom to use the power of wealth correctly. When used with restraint and wisdom, wealth can help us to become greater than ourselves. Acts of giving and kindness help us to connect with a large suffering humanity and in the process raise our consciousness.

"Giving frees us from the familiar territory of our own needs by opening our mind to the

unexplained worlds occupied by the needs of others."

Barbara Bush

What benefactors like Warren Buffet and Bill Gates are trying to do is transcend wealth itself. They are not consumers of wealth; they lead very modest lifestyles in comparison to their wealth. They understand the transcendental nature of wealth and simply choose to give it away willingly. In the process, they become larger than themselves and will outlive their wealth. Their legacy will continue long after their wealth has vanished. They will live in the hearts of men, women and children whom they have helped.

"What we do for ourselves dies with us. What we do for others and the world remains and is immortal"

Albert Pine

Some will ask as to why we should make an effort to create wealth if the end purpose is to give it away. The answer to that question is: the process of wealth creation evolves you as a human being. It normally starts with a selfish motive but in the end, it transforms you into something bigger than your narrow self. It transforms your family and other human beings who come in your contact. You understand its transitionary nature once you possess it – its possession gives you the freedom to explore and understand new things, and the chance to help others and in the process, help yourself.

Wealth is never an end in itself: it is a means towards the greater good. Some unfortunate people lose sight of the real purpose of wealth and get consumed by greed. Ultimately, such people get destroyed by their greed. Wealth built on the foundation of greed never lasts.

It does not matter how much you give—it is the principle of giving that is important. The very act of sacrifice in order to help others who are in more need than you is transformative. It sets into motion laws of karma that will open the universe of riches to you. The act of giving is a necessity and not a luxury if you want to be truly successful in life.

The purpose of this book will be served if it helps in educating and help morph enlightened people who create wealth the right way, preserve wealth the right way and ultimately, use their wealth for the greater good of humanity. This process leads to seeking a higher purpose in life and its fulfillment. I hope and pray that to some extent, that purpose is served. If you have read to this point, I thank you with gratitude in my heart and hope you succeed in creating true wealth that helps not only you and your family but entire humanity.

If you liked the book and gained some knowledge that will be useful to you in life, then please leave an honest review to help others find this book. It will be a small effort on your part, but an act of charity that may help in changing few lives for the better. We thank you in advance for your help.

This book is about fundamental principles of wealth creation that can be applied to any business or investing strategy. At Wealth Creation Academy, we teach multitude ways to generate passive income, which includes: real estate investing, digital publishing, affiliate marketing, multi-level marketing and investing in forex, commodities, and shares by copying experienced traders that need very little of time. You may like to get started with some of the strategies depending on your budget and time.

Other Books by the Authors

Praveen Kumar has authored several bestselling books. Please visit his website **http://praveenkumarauthor.com/** for more information.

About the Authors

Praveen Kumar was abandoned by his father at the age of fourteen and joined the Navy at tender age of fifteen where education, roof and free food were guaranteed.

In order to understand the root cause of suffering he turned towards philosophy and religion. After 10 years of soul searching and meditation he understood that 'life is 'and material and spiritual world are closely interwoven. You cannot live in one without the other.

Praveen was highly successful in the Navy, where he successfully commanded submarines, sailed around the world in a yacht and received gallantry award for his contribution to the Navy.

Despite his success in the Navy, Praveen realized that lack of financial security for his family was one of key root causes of his suffering, resulting from his childhood deprivation. To improve his financial standing, Praveen took pre-mature retirement from the Navy to build his financial future through investing in Real Estate. The decision to educate on financial matters paid off, and today he and his wife are comfortably retired on six-figure passive income.

His aim is to help others create wealth in an enlightened way and empower them to live a healthy and happy life. He dedicates his time to write books and articles on financial and spiritual matters.

Prashant graduated with distinction from Auckland University as a computer engineer and later completed his MBA from the world's leading institution - INSEAD. During his successful corporate career, he worked for the most reputable consulting firms in the world - BCG & Deloitte - and represented New Zealand on Prime Minister-led trade missions to South East Asian countries.

After successfully generating income through his passive investments in property and stocks, Prashant decided to team up with his father to help people transform their lives through the leverage of financial education.

Their website http://wealth-creation-academy.com/ is devoted to teaching people how to create Multiple Streams of Passive Income through investing in real estate, online marketing and creating digital products